How To Start Your Own Business Without Capital

I0493425

HTeBooks

Copyright © 2016

Disclaimer

This book is designed to provide condensed information. It is not intended to reprint all the information that is otherwise available, but instead to complement, amplify and supplement other texts. You are urged to read all the available material, learn as much as possible and tailor the information to your individual needs.

Every effort has been made to make this book as complete and as accurate as possible. However, there may be mistakes, both typographical and in content. Therefore, this text should be used only as a general guide and not as the ultimate source of information. The purpose of this book is to educate.

The author or the publisher shall have neither liability nor responsibility to any person or entity with respect to any loss or damage caused, or alleged to have been caused, directly or indirectly, by the information contained in this book.

Table of Contents

How Will This Book Help You?

From no matter what angle, businesses will always need capital. It is the one main obstacle that prevents any idea from taking flight.

The struggle of finding capital is just as complex as managing an already-established business. There are many factors to consider, obstacles to overcome, requirements to obtain, paperwork to finish so on and so forth. These variables can be very confusing and may often intimidate some of the most motivated people.

But for the truly determined, such as yourself, there is always a way. You're looking at that way right now.

This book is a guide through some of the common ways through which entrepreneurs secure capital so that their projects take flight.

When you look at capital from a larger perspective, it's a small stepping stone to even bigger possibilities. The problem only lies in how you want to go about it.

This book will show you how to go about raising funds for your business. Fast.

We all know that time is of the essence. The more time you take brooding over the possibility of failure, the sooner other people will get their own ideas in the air and probably profit off of what should have been your brainchild!

Luckily, you've already done the first step of your grand business plan; which is to read this book. From it you will learn what it takes to get the money that you need for lift off. When that happens, the rest is history; rich history.

Each chapter will discuss a source or method of obtaining capital for your business. There will also be discussions about what you need to do in order to take advantage of these sources. Be sure to take notes and stop once in a while to customize the information in this book to your business model.

At the end of each chapter is a question which will help you synthesize the information you've just received and turn it into an applicable game plan for your situation. Be sure to give the question some thought. It will help you better digest the information in the chapter that follows it.

The author would also like to point out that the methods of raising capital inside this book are not the only ways to start a business without capital. There are a lot of other methods available to the determined business owner. The methods listed here are known to be the most popular and safest ways.

Happy reading!

So you have an idea. That's all 'ya got?

"Ideas are easy. Implementation is hard."

- Guy Kawasaki

Guy Kawasaki couldn't have said it better. Humans generate ideas all the time. You must have had a hundred ideas over the course of the day. Some might have come up in the shower. Other ideas may have come to you on the way to the office. Some might have even showed up right in the middle of "taking care of business".

As you read this book, you already have a business idea in mind. There's no doubt about it. And it can also be assumed that you're pretty excited about that idea.

Whatever that business idea is, it's not enough. Don't misunderstand, though. Every business all started with an idea. But before you can turn that idea into profit, you need a few more things.

Capital is one of them.

Unless you already have the money in your hands, you're going to need investments, donations or even pledges in order to fuel the fire that is your ambition.

Most successful businessmen use the term "bootstrapping" to refer to the act of self-financing. It's not a bad way to go as well; as long as you already have the resources. But what if you don't?

What do you have that's going to connect your idea to the money you need for take-off?

A proposal, that's what you need.

Remember, you're the only one who believes in your idea at this point. There is no doubt in your firm belief on how good it's going to be.

So the next thing you have to do is to convince other people that your idea is good! *People with the money to start your idea.*

This is where your implementation comes in. The only way to present a business idea to business-oriented people is through a proposal.

A proposal could be anything from a business letter to a Powerpoint presentation to bunch of figures written on paper in a coffee shop. Proposals happen when a person with the business idea (you) approaches the people with the means to make that idea workable (them).

But no matter what the venue of your proposal may be, you can bet your million-dollar idea that every proposal has a certain set of characteristics in order to convince your potential source of capital.

The elements of a proposal

A proposal should be customized. Investors and businesses hate generic approaches. When you give them a generic letter, you get a generic answer. Those answers are usually negative in nature. When you've found a source of capital (there'll be more of that later), you need to do your homework. Who are they? How do you think your idea is going to benefit them? What can they possibly get out of funding your idea? How different is your idea from anything else they've seen? What they've done? The responsibility of due diligence falls on the entrepreneur's shoulders. When you have a customized approach, your potential investors will see how determined and convinced you are of your idea. They'll have no other choice but to agree with you on the point that your idea is a profitable one!

A proposal should be quantifiable. Business is all about money. Money is all about numbers. Therefore, your proposal should have numbers in them. In fact, your whole business idea should be translated into numbers. Using your knowledge of your potential client, you should be able to show them how much money they can make out of your idea. That means you should already have a prepared expense sheet to let them know where their money is going. On top of that, you need to be honest about your costs so that things are transparent. Avoid using vague and descriptive terms like amazing and wonderful and profitable and wealthy. The best way for a business-minded person to see your point is if you show them exactly how much you're talking about.

A proposal should be specific and straight-to-the-point. Face it. People in business have heard all the sales talk in the world. The most successful business owners might have done some selling on their own. They know it when someone is trying to sweet-talk them into a deal. That will make your proposal insincere and devious. At best, simply state what you plan to do and let their imaginations do the rest. "Here's what I do. Here's how much you can make. Here's what I need to make that happen. I'd be happy to answer any questions you might have." Simple. Powerful.

While you don't have any investors to impress at the moment, the best thing you should do is to work on your proposal. This will give you a better image of what you have to offer. It will also show you the weaknesses of your idea and provide you some time to work out those bugs.

One important thing you have to remember is that the goal of a proposal is to *get your investors to have the same enthusiasm you have about your idea.*

*)When you have a great idea, you need to give it form and shape. The best form to give an idea is the form of a proposal that is customized, specific and quantifiable. The best way to create such a person is to ask yourself "Would I want to fund my own idea if I had the money?"

Method 1: Bank Financing

"A boy becomes a man when he stops asking his father for money and requests a loan."

- Unknown

Usually, the first place to look for money is a place that lends money to people. What better place to look for than a bank?

But with culture and neighbor's stories and TV news, banks haven't had a very good reputation for the striving entrepreneur. There's a lot of good and bad going around and it is quite difficult to make heads or tails of whether or not to go to a bank for a loan.

Allow the author of this book to put this out in the air: A bank is a business.

Banks operate in order to make money, not give money out. That's what charitable foundations are for. Going back to your idea, ask yourself this question:

"Is my idea supposed to make me money?"

If the answer to that question is yes, then a bank is a good place to go to for a loan to make your business idea take off. Get rid of the notion that banks are evil and just want to take all your money. There are laws that stipulate what banks can and cannot do. They are business establishments just as much as any other company out there in the market right now.

How does it work?

Different banks have different loan programs that are designed for people who want to start their own business. One thing that you have to remember that for whatever type of loan you're going to apply for, you'll always need a proposal.

You may not directly have to make an appeal or proposal to the bank. In most cases, you have to go though the SBA. That's known as the small business association. This organization will take care of approving you for a loan. These are the people who need to see what you have under your sleeve. Time to whip out that proposal!

Don't get your hopes up too high though. It's very rare that the SBA approves the full amount that you need. The highest you can get is about 80% of what you're asking if you get approved. That isn't bad though. That only leaves you to find another source for the remaining 20%.

Another good thing about going through the SBA is that you'll get a good idea of how business organizations and investors will see your proposal. Think of it as a dry run of your business idea. They may be able to tell you what other people might see as problems with your business model which will help you improve on your idea.

When the SBA approves your loan, they'll give you documentation that authorizes you to apply for a bank loan. The next step after that is to apply for your loans from an actual bank. When the bank approves it, you get the money.

Upon the release of the capital, you'll have to pay them back. Depending on the interest rates, you'll be paying them more than what they lent you in the first place. The sooner you can pay them back, the lower the interest you have to pay.

Advantages

Other sources of capital force you to surrender part of your ownership to them in exchange for their money. This is known as equity. This may cause your idea to change in ways that you might not have thought of, or approved of. You won't have full control over how your business is run and you'll have to share your profit. Through a bank loan, you get none of that. All you have is a time frame within which you have to pay back your debt.

Disadvantages

Bank loans can be double-edged swords if not used wisely. With a loan comes debt. This could happen if your idea does not sell. If the business flops, you'll end up with a debt that you may not be able to pay with your current job. That may put you in a worse position from when you started. And even when your business takes off and you start seeing profit, most of it will go to paying off that loan. That means a delay in your ROI or return of investment.

*)A Bank loan is one of the most direct ways to raise funds for your business. It can also be a gamble. Are you confident enough in your idea to take out a loan?

Method 2: Credit Cards

"Procrastination is like a credit card: it's a lot of fun until you get the bill."

- Christopher Parker

Separate from banking, credit cards are another way to secure the things that you need in order to get your project started. Instead of taking out a loan from the bank, you charge your business expenses to your credit card.

During the period of 1990 -2000, one of the largest IT companies in the world was started using credit cards. It was Google. The two founders built an empire on a good credit rating. The results are as you see today. During the foundation of the company within their garage, the founders maxed out their credit cards and made good use of the purchases they made. This helped them recover from their credit card bills and create a business that would later become a household name.

How does it work?

It's just as straight-forward as taking out a bank loan. But this time, you do all the spending on your own. You buy your materials, you take out cash on credit to pay for labor as well as hire your own people. Just like any other expense that your credit card can cover, they will also be subject to the laws that credit cards have. The longer you take to pay the charges, the higher the interest rate.

There is also a limit to the amount that can be charged unto a card at a certain time. This amount strongly depends on the kind of credit card you have and your credit score.

Your credit score is a rating provided by the Credit Bureau to rate how good of a debt-payer you are. The higher the credit rating, the more credit you can use. Think of it as buying for things using your reputation. When you fail to pay your credit card bills, this affects your credit score. A bad credit rating means that you're not allowed to use credit and you would need to reestablish yourself with a good payment history. That can take some time. Try to consult different credit card companies and see what sorts of business cards they can provide you with.

Advantages

This is one of the quickest ways to get started as you don't need anyone else's support. You only have your credit score to help you. If you already have a credit card, you can get started on getting the things you need to start your business. There's no equity, you can keep all the profits that your business generates and best of all, you don't share control with anyone.

Disadvantages

While there is convenience in using a credit card, that convenience comes at a steep price. Credit card companies use higher interest rates compared to bank loans. You're looking at rates that go above 20%. That means you'll be paying exponentially higher bills if you pay them off at a later date. You would need to get your returns and profit sooner if you want to settle your bill. Most experts advise that you keep this method as a last resort if your other efforts to secure capital prove fruitless.

*)Operating on your credit score, you can amass the necessities you need to get your idea to materialize. When was the last time you checked your credit score? Try applying for a credit card and see what the credit card companies have to say about your credit score.

Method 3: Crowdfunding

"People paying you for doing what you love is different than finding more people who love what you do."

- Jack Conte

This new and interesting way of getting funding still hasn't reached its boom yet. But from the way that crowdfunding is getting great ideas out in the open, it's sure to get its time soon enough.

How does it work?

Traditional methods of getting loans and investments have people making proposals to one investor at a time, asking for a large amount of money to cover all the expenses. With crowdfunding, you do the same things in reverse!

Ask for small amounts of money from many people

One large question a lot of people ask will be how to do such a thing. If you tried crowdfunding before the advent of the internet, it would have been almost impossible and impractical.

But through the reach of the internet, creative people and entrepreneurs are now placing their projects on an online platform to share their ideas with people who want to back them up. And they're getting things done.

There are a few websites through which you can do this. There's Kickstart and Gofundme. These websites offer a space through which people share their project ideas and ask to support their efforts.

All users have to do is to create an account and place their proposals there. Given that this is the internet, proposals go a lot differently.

Instead of displaying long texts and Powerpoint presentations, people now use visuals and Youtube videos to show what they want to achieve. When it comes to marketing over the internet, you want to keep things short and loud. You may want to start developing your video editing skills if you want to give this a try.

These websites offer donation and pledge methods that will allow most users to make payments towards these projects. In exchange for donations and pledges, users can select rewards from the entrepreneur based on how much they donate. These rewards are usually product samples of the project idea.

Each project is given a time-frame and a goal before it receives payout from the funding.

Instead of getting loans and grants, you get donations, pledges and payments. These will come in very small amounts and they will come one at a time. That's the reason it's called crowdfunding. You're getting funds from a crowd.

Advantages

Unlike other traditional methods, this fund raising method doesn't cost as much. All you need are a few samples and you can entice people to back your project. If you're planning on selling products, you can reward your investors with samples and freebies and discounts.

You'll also be reaching a lot of people in shorter spans of time. If you understand your target market, your product and your goals, you can go beyond your targets.

Despite these advantages, the best thing about crowdfunding is that if your idea is good enough and your presentation is convincing, *you may end up with more capital than you initially thought you wanted.* Some of the best Kickstart projects went way over their initial asking price and are now big names in their industries.

Are you familiar with the Pebble Watch? That Bluetooth-capable watch that synchs with your smartphone or iphone and can use different watch faces? That was a Kickstart project. The amazing thing about this story is that they only needed an initial start of $100,000. They ended up with $10,000,000.

Another popular product of crowdfunding is the Occulus Rift. This is a virtual gaming system that promised to give games a full 3d gaming experience that immerses them right into the action. When this project started, they only asked for$250,000 but they ended up raising $2,000,000 by the time their funding ended.

There are hundreds of other examples out there, waiting to be discovered. Your idea might just be the next big thing on the internet.

Disadvantages

Although the internet can be a great place to start, it can also be a great place to fail. Because of the anonymity that the internet provides, your idea could fall prey to people who simply want to put you down. Your project may get the limelight or the harsh criticisms of netizens who might not be as enthusiastic about your idea as you are. There's also the possibility of you not being able to make your target amount by the time your campaign ends because of lack of interest and buzz.

Basically, to do business on the internet, you need to create a buzz for your idea. You have to get people to start talking about it. Unlike traditional methods wherein you only had to convince a small group of people or even just one person, crowdfunding puts you up on a stage for the whole world to see. This is done through social media channels such as Facebook and Twitter. And you have to get everyone's short attention long enough in order for them to give you a second look. In short, it all depends on the likability of your idea and the attractiveness of your presentation.

*)Raising capital through crowdfunding uses the myriad contributions of plenty people in order to come up with a sum large enough to start the business. How much money

do you think you need to start? From what kinds of people do you think your project will gather the most attention?

Method 4: Venture Capital

"Remember that nobodies are the new somebodies."

- Guy Kawasaki

You hear this term a lot during seminars and entrepreneurial conventions. It's an interesting industry that involves people who want to make money and people who have ideas that are going to make money.

How does it work?

Venture capital is referred to as investments made by venture capitalists into start-ups that show potential. In short, it's where the entrepreneur and the creditor both benefit from the partnership.

Also called "co-founding" in some instances, venture capital doesn't only put money and ideas together. In other cases, entrepreneurs also come after the expertise of the venture capitalists when it comes to management and business development. With that said, venture capitalists are entitled to equity shares of the start-up.

What makes venture capital different from other forms of fund raising is that the venture capitalist can have more than one venture under their sleeve. They choose the businesses they want to help and they assist in helping them grow. They do this not just with their money but also with their knowledge and manpower.

There are numerous VC firms and specialists out in the market right now. You can freely do a Google search and pull up a long list of names of people you might find willing to help fund your project. Don't forget to customize your proposals and presentations for them. They can smell a generic and lazy presentation from a mile away.

Some of the more known names in the market include Guy Kawasaki and Saar Gur:

Lately, it has been noted that venture capitalists prefer investing in ideas with the following characteristics:

Innovative technology – Take note that these people are game changers. They are thrilled by ideas that can disrupt the current system and bring about great improvements to society. This makes IT projects very attractive to them. If your idea has something to do with technology, you have a good chance of getting venture capital.

Potential for rapid growth – After seeing so many business models and failures and successes around them, venture capitalists have developed a nose for ideas that have the potential to boom in the market. Even if your idea is turned down by a venture capitalist, you're sure to get expert opinion on making your idea more irresistible.

A well-developed business model – If there's one thing that business-minded people hate, it's getting down and dirty with the details. They want to make a big decision and have their people take care of the nitty-gritty. If you approach a venture capitalist with a great idea but a vague model, they won't waste time making a model for you. You need to figure out a working system that benefits both you and your co-founder in order to get a 'yes' from them.

Advantages

As said earlier, you don't just get capital to start your business. You get expertise. You'll be dealing with people who see more than 15 proposals before coffee break on a bad day. No amount of capital can match that kind of knowledge helping your business grow. On top of that, dealing with venture capitalists will give you a good idea on the possible demand for your product. That kind of insight only comes with time and exposure, something a start-up doesn't have.

Disadvantages

This is a model that entails equity. You'll be giving part of your control over to someone else besides you. The problem with this is that people can change. Your preferences and ideals might change as well. You might end up having more disagreements than agreements with your co-founder and you might just end up giving 15% of your company away on the market. You could have had that share to yourself.

On top of that, approaching venture capitalists can be a bit tricky as well. The research involved is no joke. You'll have to look at who they handled, the kind of industry their firm specializes in, what they're looking for, what their business strategies are and a lot of other factors that can either make or break your proposal.

*)With venture capital, both you and your co founder are going to engage in a relationship wherein you provide the idea, they provide the capital and knowledge. How big of a portion of your equity are you going to give your co-founder?

Method 5: Friends and Family

"I know I can always count on my family."

- Homer Simpson

Ideally, the best people to help your business grow are the people who want to see you grow personally as well. This is where your friends and family come in. There are plenty of businesses built upon a family with shared investments in the business. Many experts say that they're a good place to start if you have nowhere else to go. Don't overlook it!

How does it work?

Simply enough, you just have to explain your idea to your family and friends and show them what they can get out of it. Remember, you're convincing your loved ones. They'll know if you're sincere or not. If you have strong faith in your idea, then they will feel it and know that you're on to something.

Advantages

One of the most obvious benefits of raising capital from family and friends is that you're more comfortable talking to them about your ideas. Your thoughts will come across better if you speak to people who know you inside-out. They'll also be able to give you their honest opinions about your plans.

On top of that, you're also exposing yourself to different points of view from different people. Depending on which industry your relatives work for, you can get perspectives from all kinds of directions.

Finally, the success of your idea will not just benefit you, but your whole family. Their investment in your idea will also help them financially and emotionally.

Disadvantages

If the gains are big, so are the risks. Mixing business matters in family discussions can be frustrating. Talking about money within the family also puts undue stress on your loved ones.

When your business hits a low, you can be sure that your family and friends are going to feel it. You may be a part of the family, but they're your investors nonetheless. Your failures become their failures. Even when you incur losses due to factors that are out of your control, you'll still feel responsible for not putting their money to good use.

In order to lessen the burden, be sure that you're borrowing disposable income instead of savings. That way, the burden is lighter and you feel less stressed when your business hits lows, especially in the earlier stages after take-off.

*)Raising Funds through your family and friends is one of the most accessible options you have as an entrepreneur. Will you convince them the same way you would an investor? What things would you change?

Method 6: A Second Mortgage

"There are mortgages on every castle in the air."

- Unknown

You may have thought about it already. It's not a bad idea. Getting a second mortgage on your house could be the idea that you're looking for.

For the beginner, mortgages are a type of loan that you get in return for your house. You don't necessarily have to move out when you get it, but you have to pay it off in due time lest the creditor seizes your home.

But when it comes to business, some people find it worth their while to get a second mortgage if it means they can get their idea of the ground.

How does it work?

You can also call them home equity lines of credit. Instead of giving up the equity of your potential business, business owners can choose to give up a portion of their property instead of a portion of their company.

Advantages

One of the brighter sides of this is that you'll enjoy lower interest rates. Take note that you're not running on your credit score. You're betting on your actual property that your idea is going to be a hit. When it does happen, you'll have less of a mortgage to worry about.

The lower interest rates come from the fact that the creditors can seize your home if you fail payments, so be careful.

Another good thing about this is that because you're not offering up equity in exchange for capital, you're going to own 100% of your company.

Disadvantages

As mentioned earlier, you're putting your property on the line. This still represents a risk. If you're willing to take the risk, make sure you have a back-up plan.

On top of this, you may not get as much as you would have hoped for. For second mortgages, creditors may only end up giving you as low as three-fourths of the market price of your property. Although this may put you in a rears a bit, many have been known to start businesses on a second mortgage.

*)Getting a second mortgage means putting your property in the hands of your lenders. If you were to take out one, how much would you think you would obtain from such a transaction?

How to Apply What You've Learned?

Go over the methods and see which one fits your business idea best. Be sure to take a look at these considerations:

Will the people I'm approaching be receptive to the way I present my ideas? What is the best way to show them that my idea will work?

Depending on my target market, which investor/fundraising method will work best for me?

What resources do I already have? Do I need a lot more or do I simply need a little more push in the right direction?

How much am I going to need? Do I need plenty of equipment? Am I going to have to hire people to work for me? How much am I going to pay them?

How profitable is my idea? How soon can I expect a return on my investment?

Answering these questions will give you a better insight as to how your potential investors will respond to your proposal.

The information provided for each method is merely the tip of the iceberg. Depending on the investor/institution/firm you approach, you might encounter new ideas and methods or even obstacles that will either help or hinder you from raising the funds that you need. Be sure to observe and take plenty of notes. This is especially handy after a discussion with an investor. The more information you have, the more educated choices you can make in the future.

Finally, keep in mind that rejection is part of any struggle. As much as you would hope that your idea will take flight immediately, you are going to meet resistance. Plenty of it. There will be people who are not going to agree without and there are people who are going to de-motivate you. Some will even mock you for trying. What's important is that you still persist.

Most venture capitalists find themselves disappointed by the lack of persistency coming from entrepreneurs. After 12 months of not having answer, they quit their efforts and waste even more of their time. Any business expert will agree with you if you say that persistency is the key to business. You will definitely get your share of hard times. It's how you respond to these challenges that make you a worthy investment.

www.ingramcontent.com/pod-product-compliance
Lightning Source LLC
Chambersburg PA
CBHW070229210526
45169CB00023B/1516